Families Today

TEEN PARENTS

Families Today

Adoptive Families

Disability and Families

Foster Families

Homelessness and Families

Immigrant Families

Incarceration and Families

LGBT Families

Military Families

Multigenerational Families

Multiracial Families

Single-Parent Families

Teen Parents

Families Today

TEEN PARENTS

H.W. Poole

MASON CREST
SANDUSKY LIBRARY

Mason Crest
450 Parkway Drive, Suite D
Broomall, PA 19008
www.masoncrest.com

© 2017 by Mason Crest, an imprint of National Highlights, Inc. All rights reserved. No part of this publication may be reproduced or transmitted in any form or by any means, electronic or mechanical, including photocopying, recording, taping, or any information storage and retrieval system, without permission from the publisher.

MTM Publishing, Inc.
435 West 23rd Street, #8C
New York, NY 10011
www.mtmpublishing.com

President: Valerie Tomaselli
Vice President, Book Development: Hilary Poole
Designer: Annemarie Redmond
Copyeditor: Peter Jaskowiak
Editorial Assistant: Andrea St. Aubin

Series ISBN: 978-1-4222-3612-3
Hardback ISBN: 978-1-4222-3624-6
E-Book ISBN: 978-1-4222-8268-7

Library of Congress Cataloging-in-Publication Data
Names: Poole, Hilary W., author.
Title: Teen parents / by H.W. Poole.
Description: Broomall, PA : Mason Crest [2017] | Series: Families Today | Includes index.
Identifiers: LCCN 2016004546| ISBN 9781422236246 (hardback) | ISBN 9781422236123 (series) | ISBN 9781422282687 (e-book)
Subjects: LCSH: Teenage parents—Juvenile literature. | Teenage mothers—Juvenile literature. | Teenagers—Sexual behavior—Juvenile literature. | Families—Juvenile literature.
Classification: LCC HQ759.64 .P66 2017 | DDC 306.874/3—dc23
LC record available at http://lccn.loc.gov/2016004546

Printed and bound in the United States of America.

First printing
9 8 7 6 5 4 3 2 1

TABLE OF CONTENTS

Series Introduction 7
Chapter One: Teens and Sexual Activity .11
Chapter Two: Being Pregnant 21
Chapter Three: Special Concerns for Teen Moms 29
Chapter Four: Being a Mom, Being a Dad. 37
Further Reading 44
Series Glossary 45
Index 47
About the Author 48
Photo Credits 48

Key Icons to Look for:

Words to Understand: These words with their easy-to-understand definitions will increase the reader's understanding of the text, while building vocabulary skills.

Sidebars: This boxed material within the main text allows readers to build knowledge, gain insights, explore possibilities, and broaden their perspectives by weaving together additional information to provide realistic and holistic perspectives.

Research Projects: Readers are pointed toward areas of further inquiry connected to each chapter. Suggestions are provided for projects that encourage deeper research and analysis.

Text-Dependent Questions: These questions send the reader back to the text for more careful attention to the evidence presented there.

Series Glossary of Key Terms: This back-of-the-book glossary contains terminology used throughout the series. Words found here increase the reader's ability to read and comprehend higher-level books and articles in this field.

In the 21st century, families are more diverse than ever before.

SERIES INTRODUCTION

Our vision of "the traditional family" is not nearly as time-honored as one might think. The standard of a mom, a dad, and a couple of kids in a nice house with a white-picket fence is a relic of the 1950s—the heart of the baby boom era. The tumult of the Great Depression followed by a global war caused many Americans to long for safety and predictability—whether such stability was real or not. A newborn mass media was more than happy to serve up this image, in the form of TV shows like *Leave It To Beaver* and *The Adventures of Ozzie and Harriet*. Interestingly, even back in the "glory days" of the traditional family, things were never as simple as they seemed. For example, a number of the classic "traditional" family shows—such as *The Andy Griffith Show, My Three Sons,* and a bit later, *The Courtship of Eddie's Father*—were actually focused on single-parent families.

Sure enough, by the 1960s our image of the "perfect family" was already beginning to fray at the seams. The women's movement, the gay rights movement, and—perhaps more than any single factor—the advent of "no fault" divorce meant that the illusion of the Cleaver family would become harder and harder to maintain. By the early 21st century, only about 7 percent of all family households were traditional—defined as a married couple with children where *only* the father works outside the home.

As the number of these traditional families has declined, "nontraditional" arrangements have increased. There are more single parents, more gay and lesbian parents, and more grandparents raising grandchildren than ever before. Multiracial families—created either through interracial relationships or adoption—are also increasing. Meanwhile, the transition to an all-volunteer military force has meant that there are more kids growing up in military families than there were in the past. Each of these topics is treated in a separate volume in this set.

While some commentators bemoan the decline of the traditional family, others argue that, overall, the recognition of new family arrangements has brought more good than bad. After all, if very few people live like the Cleavers anyway, isn't it better to be honest about that fact? Surely, holding up the traditional family as an ideal to which all should aspire only serves to stigmatize kids whose lives differ from that standard. After all, no children can be held responsible for whatever family they find themselves in; all they can do is grow up as best they can. These books take the position that every family—no matter what it looks like—has the potential to be a successful family.

That being said, challenges and difficulties arise in every family, and nontraditional ones are no exception. For example, single parents tend to be less well off financially than married parents are, and this has long-term impacts on their children. Meanwhile, teenagers who become parents tend to let their educations suffer, which damages their income potential and career possibilities, as well as risking the future educational attainment of their babies. There are some 400,000 children in the foster care system at any given time. We know that the uncertainty of foster care creates real challenges when it comes to both education and emotional health.

Furthermore, some types of "nontraditional" families are ones we wish did not have to exist at all. For example, an estimated 1.6 million children experience homelessness at some point in their lives. At least 40 percent of homeless kids are lesbian, gay, bisexual, or transgender teens who were turned out of their homes because of their orientation. Meanwhile, the United States incarcerates more people than any other nation in the world—about 2.7 million kids (1 in 28) have an incarcerated parent. It would be absurd to pretend that such situations are not extremely stressful and, often, detrimental to kids who have to survive them.

The goal of this set, then, is twofold. First, we've tried to describe the history and shape of various nontraditional families in such a way that kids who aren't familiar with them will be able to not only understand, but empathize. We also present demographic information that may be useful for students who are dipping their toes into introductory sociology concepts.

Second, we have tried to speak specifically to the young people who are living in these nontraditional families. The series strives to address these kids as

Meeting challenges and overcoming them together can make families stronger.

sympathetically and supportively as possible. The volumes look at some of the typical problems that kids in these situations face, and where appropriate, they offer advice and tips for how these kids might get along better in whatever situation confronts them.

Obviously, no single book—whether on disability, the military, divorce, or some other topic—can hope to answer every question or address every problem. To that end, a "Further Reading" section at the back of each book attempts to offer some places to look next. We have also listed appropriate crisis hotlines, for anyone with a need more immediate than can be addressed by a library.

Whether your students have a project to complete or a problem to solve, we hope they will be able to find clear, empathic information about nontraditional families in these pages.

—H. W. Poole

Teen Parents

The decision to become sexually active can have life-changing consequences.

Chapter One

TEENS AND SEXUAL ACTIVITY

The media often scares parents with stories about all the terrible or dangerous things their kids might be secretly doing. But in reality, fewer kids commit crimes, do drugs, or have sex than the news suggests. For example, recent surveys have shown that about 7 in 10 kids between the ages of 15 and 17 have never had sexual intercourse.

Of course, if about 70 percent are not having sex, that still means that about 30 percent of kids that age *are*—and that's still a large number. Teens who do choose to have sex need to understand the possible consequences. First, there are almost always emotional consequences to sex. The act of intercourse is more of a "big deal" than a lot kids expect it will be. There can also be

Words to Understand

abortion: a medical procedure that ends a pregnancy.

abstinence: choosing to not do something (in this context, have sex).

comprehensive: covering all aspects of a topic.

contraception: something a person uses to prevent pregnancy.

miscarriage: when an unborn baby does not survive.

health consequences. Just because a sex partner is young and "looks healthy," that's actually no guarantee that he or she can't give you a sexually transmitted infection (STI).

But by far, the most significant consequence of intercourse is the creation of a new life. Teenagers who become parents—and *especially* girls who become mothers—find their lives permanently changed. Becoming a parent when you are still a kid yourself is incredibly challenging. It is vital that teenagers who find themselves in this position understand precisely what they are getting into.

TEENS AND SEX

Advertisements are designed to convince people to buy things. One classic method is to suggest that a certain product will make a person more attractive—thinner, younger, prettier, or more handsome. This approach inspired the now-common saying, "Sex sells." And it's not just advertising—sexual imagery is everywhere, including in music videos, talk shows, and fashion magazines. Meanwhile, the characters in movies and TV shows seem to be constantly pairing up for casual sex. Judging by today's media, you might think that adults never think about anything else.

This can put a lot of pressure on kids. The media hints that girls should be "sexy" at younger and younger ages. TV shows and

Using sexuality to sell products seems to happen everywhere—these mannequins were photographed in a store in Ramallah, Palestine.

Chapter One: Teens and Sexual Activity

Myths about Sex and Pregnancy

"You can't get pregnant the first time you have sex."
This is completely untrue. You can get pregnant any time you have intercourse.

"You can't get pregnant if you are having your period."
Also untrue—you are less likely to get pregnant, but it is still possible.

"It's okay to reuse condoms, or to use plastic wrap instead."
Forget it—both are highly likely to leak. This makes them ineffective contraception.

"Mountain Dew is a good contraceptive because it kills sperm."
This is not true at all! This also applies to Coke, Pepsi, and any other beverage. The ingredients in soda do not kill sperm.

"If I get pregnant, my boyfriend will love me more."
Unfortunately, this isn't always the case. Because there is so much stress involved in a pregnancy, childbirth, and the baby's first year, relationships are just as likely to suffer as they are to get better.

"If you really love me, you'll have sex with me."
No way. There are lots of ways to express love—sex is just one of them.

films create the impression that a "real" romantic relationship should involve sex right away. Kids often hear their friends brag about all the sexual adventures they are having. It can make kids who are *not* sexually active feel like freaks.

But when it comes to teens and sex, movies and rumors are not the whole story. A 2011 study found that among teenagers aged 15 to 17, more than 60 percent of girls and more than 50 percent of boys had never had *any* form of sexual contact with someone of the opposite sex. When the researchers narrowed the question to ask about sexual intercourse, the numbers dropped even lower: only 31 percent of boys and 33 percent of girls between 15 and 17 had had intercourse.

So if your friends tell you that "everybody is doing it," they are probably lying. The truth is, there is nothing wrong with choosing to wait—and in fact, you have a lot of company (even if other kids don't admit it!).

PREGNANCY BY THE NUMBERS

There is something a bit strange about discussing sexual activity in terms of statistics. After all, the decision to have or not have sex is one of the most private and personal decisions anyone can make. But because individuals all make that decision at some point, it is possible to look at a large group of those decisions and draw some conclusions. So, statistics are one way we can learn more about ourselves.

When it comes to teen pregnancy, the statistics are fascinating. When we talk about a "pregnancy rate," what we mean is the number of pregnancies per 1,000 females of a certain age. For example, out of 1,000 girls between the ages of 15 and 19, roughly 95 got pregnant in the course of 1972. In 1973, roughly 96 girls out of 1,000 got pregnant. So we would say there was a slight increase in

Pregnancy Rates versus Pregnancy Outcomes

The pregnancy rate includes all pregnancies, including those that ended in **miscarriage** or **abortion**. So pregnancy rates don't tell you how many babies were actually born. In the peak year of 1990, there were 362,800 pregnancies among girls 15 to 17; these resulted in 183,327 births and 129,820 abortions, with the remainder being miscarriages. By 2010 the number of pregnancies had dropped to an all-time low of 189,000. These pregnancies resulted in 109,173 births and 52,720 abortions—a huge drop from previous years.

Chapter One: Teens and Sexual Activity

Margaret Sanger with her infant son in 1906. Sanger was a pioneer in the fight to make birth control more accessible.

the pregnancy rate between those years. There was another increase the next year (to almost 99), and the next (to 101). In fact, the rate rose fairly steadily for almost two decades. (There was a brief leveling-off period in the 1980s.) The teen pregnancy rate peaked in 1990, when almost 117 girls out of every 1,000 became pregnant.

Among girls 14 years old and younger, the rate also rose steadily. In 1973 there were 13.5 pregnancies for every 1,000 girls of that age group. By 1990, that rate was up to 17.5. But in 1991, pregnancy rates began to decline every year. By 2000 the pregnancy rate for girls between 15 and 19 was down to 83.4 per 1,000; by 2005 it had dropped to 68.3; and by 2010 it was 57.4. That's the lowest rate ever recorded in the United States. (Rates among girls 14 and younger also declined, down to 5.4 by 2010.) Importantly, rates have dropped in all parts of the country and among all races and ethnic groups. There is no easy answer as to why this has occurred, but researchers have some general ideas.

UNDERSTANDING THE RATES

In one sense, pregnancy is easy to avoid. If you don't want to get pregnant, don't have sex. **Abstinence** is the only 100 percent effective way to steer clear of not only pregnancy but also STIs. Some schools offer "abstinence-only education,"

Teen Pregnancy around the World

While teen pregnancy rates are at historic lows in the United States, the country still lags behind many other developed nations. In 2014 the Guttmacher Institute published a study about teen pregnancy around the world in the *Journal of Adolescent Health*. The study looked at birth rates among teenagers in different countries. The study also looked at the percentage of those pregnancies that were terminated. (The data come from national statistics and from UN data.)

PREGNANCIES AND ABORTIONS AMONG 15–17-YEAR-OLDS, SELECTED COUNTRIES

Country	Year	Pregnancies per 1,000 females	Percentage ending in abortion
Switzerland	2011	8	59
Germany	2011	9	23
Japan	2010	13	53
Singapore	2011	14	54
Netherlands	2008	14	50
Croatia	2011	17	17
Lithuania	2011	19	21
Czech Republic	2011	20	33
Denmark	2011	21	67
Finland	2011	23	55
Norway	2011	23	56
France	2011	25	61

which means that while the class might cover the biological aspects of sex, the only form of **contraception** discussed is avoiding sex altogether.

But some teens, especially older ones, feel that abstinence is not right for them. Research suggests that abstinence-only education does not do much to

Chapter One: Teens and Sexual Activity

PREGNANCIES AND ABORTIONS AMONG 15–17-YEAR-OLDS, SELECTED COUNTRIES

Country	Year	Pregnancies per 1,000 females	Percentage ending in abortion
Spain	2011	26	50
Canada	2011	28	42
Sweden	2010	29	69
Iceland	2011	30	51
Slovakia	2011	33	17
Hungary	2011	38	41
Estonia	2011	43	43
Ukraine	2011	44	21
Scotland	2011	46	37
England and Wales	2011	47	42
Russian Federation	2011	49	34
New Zealand	2011	51	36
Kyrgyzstan*	2011	57	11
United States	2010	57	26
Romania	2011	61	28
Ethiopia*	2008	121	9
Mexico*	2009	130	34
Malawi*	2009	154	14
Kenya*	2012	174	22

Notes: Years included are the most recent ones where data were available; Germany includes abortions for 17-year-olds only.

* Abortion rates are based on country studies that estimate the numbers through indirect measurement.

Source: Gilda Sedgh et al., "Adolescent Pregnancy, Birth, and Abortion Rates Across Countries: Levels and Recent Trends," Journal of Adolescent Health 56 (2015): 223–230. http://www.jahonline.org/article/S1054-139X(14)00387-5/pdf.

change teen behavior. Although more than $1.5 billion has been spent to fund abstinence-only programs, it has not been proven that the programs influence teens to make different sexual decisions. For example, a 2007 study found that kids who had taken an abstinence-only class did not wait any longer to have sex than kids who had not taken the class. States such as Arizona, Texas, Pennsylvania, and Kansas studied their abstinence-only programs and found that the classes did not change the students' opinions about whether or not to have sex. Another study found that kids who take "virginity pledges," where they promise not to have sex until marriage, actually only wait about 18 months longer than kids who don't take the pledge. A greater concern is that virginity pledge-takers are less likely to use condoms than other kids, and they also have STIs at slightly higher rates.

This evidence suggests that abstinence programs are not the reason for the decline in teen pregnancy rates. Instead, researchers point to an increasing use of contraception among teenagers. Doctors have become more willing to prescribe birth control pills to teenagers. Young people have become more willing to use condoms and other methods. More **comprehensive** sex education programs (unlike abstinence-only programs) have been shown to change teens'

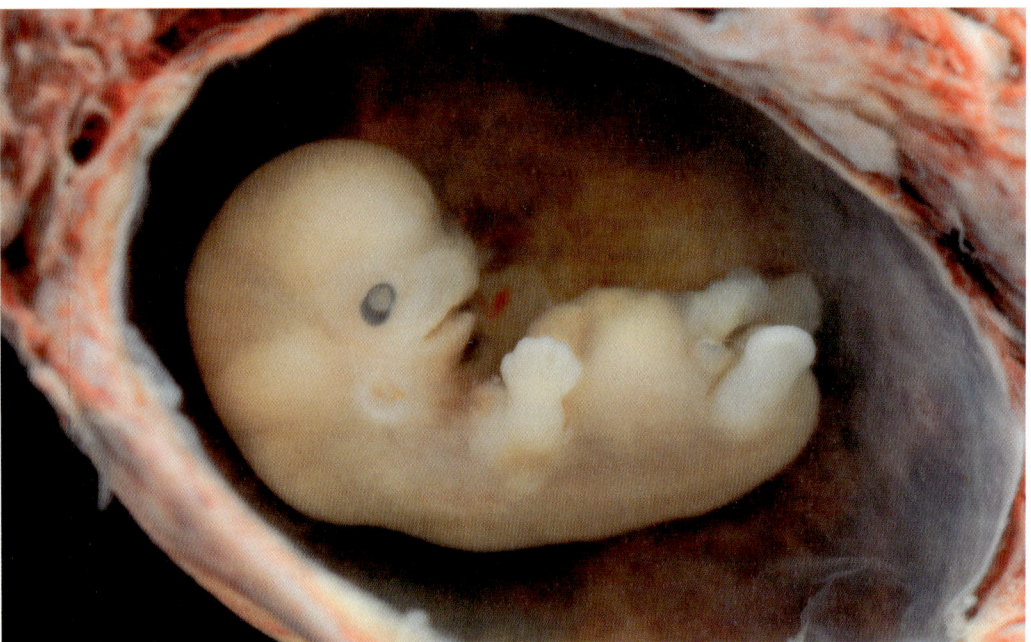

A developing baby goes through huge changes during the 40 weeks of pregnancy. This image shows a fetus at about 8 weeks.

Chapter One: Teens and Sexual Activity

attitudes about using contraception. Meanwhile, there has been a nationwide trend toward postponing children until women are a bit older. This general trend has probably also affected how teens view the risk of pregnancy.

Heather D. Boonstra of the Guttmacher Institute (a main source of information about reproductive health) wrote, "At the end of the day, the credit for the declines in teen pregnancy goes to adolescents themselves, how they are making an effort to prevent unintended pregnancy."

A doctor or nurse can explain how the menstrual cycle works and provide information about different birth-control options.

Text-Dependent Questions

1. What is the percentage of teens aged 15 to 17 who are not having sex?
2. What are some myths about getting pregnant, and what is the truth?
3. Why do experts think the teen pregnancy rate has gone down?

Research Project

Find out what type of sex education is available in your school. Interview a teacher or school counselor about why that particular type of sex education is used.

Teen Parents

A surprise pregnancy can strain relationships, but the parents-to-be can also be great supports to each other.

Chapter Two

BEING PREGNANT

Sometimes people decide to have sex but do not take precautions to avoid pregnancy. Other times, they take bad precautions (see sidebar on myths, page 13), and still other times, they do an excellent job of taking precautions, but the young woman ends up pregnant anyway. Accidents do happen.

When a teenage girl discovers she is pregnant, she might feel a wide range of emotions, often all at the same time: fear, excitement, anger, confusion, worry… maybe even embarrassment or shame. She might also feel a little sick, because the physical changes of pregnancy often upset the stomach.

Words to Understand

anemia: a condition in which the blood does not have enough red blood cells; causes exhaustion, dizziness, and other symptoms; can be fatal in extreme cases.

expectant: in this case, pregnant.

pain management: various methods of helping a patient handle the pain he or she is in.

prenatal: before birth.

DON'T GO IT ALONE

Discovering you are pregnant can be overwhelming. There's a big temptation to pretend the pregnancy isn't happening. This is understandable, but it is unwise. The baby is going to grow and develop, whether the **expectant** mom likes it or not. Facing reality is the first step toward making the situation better.

A pregnant teen needs to find an adult she can trust. It needs to be someone who can help her handle the many challenges she's about to face. Hopefully, that person is her mom or dad. It's common for parents to be quite upset at the news. Getting pregnant at a young age is not a dream that most parents have for their daughters. But after they calm down and accept reality, most parents will put their own feelings aside and help their kids sort things out.

Unfortunately, some teens don't feel like they can trust their parents, for whatever reason. In these cases, it is vital that they find some other adult who can help. It could be an aunt, grandmother, or other relative, or it could be a teacher, minister, or coach. There are also trained counselors who can help teen moms.

BIG DECISIONS

There are a number of important questions that a pregnant teen needs to consider immediately. A full discussion of these issues is outside the scope of this book. But just quickly, those questions include:

How involved will the father be? Young men who decide to have sex should expect to deal with the consequences. But not all teenage boys are mature enough to handle this situation. What and when to tell the young man (and his family) is a tricky matter that varies greatly from person to person. (For more on teen dads, see page 38.)

Will the pregnancy continue or be terminated? Abortion is an extremely controversial topic in the United States, and many people have very strong feelings about it. That said, abortion is a legal procedure and teenagers have the right to consider it.

Will she give the baby up for adoption or raise it herself? Again, this is a hugely complex decision, and there is no wrong answer. It depends entirely on the specifics of each individual girl's situation.

PRENATAL CARE

Pregnant teens are more likely than pregnant women to have a variety of problems, such as **anemia** and high blood pressure. Their babies are more likely than average to be born prematurely, and at low birth weights. These problems set the stage for their babies to have developmental problems later in life. A major cause of these problems is that pregnant teens do not always get the **prenatal** medical care that they need.

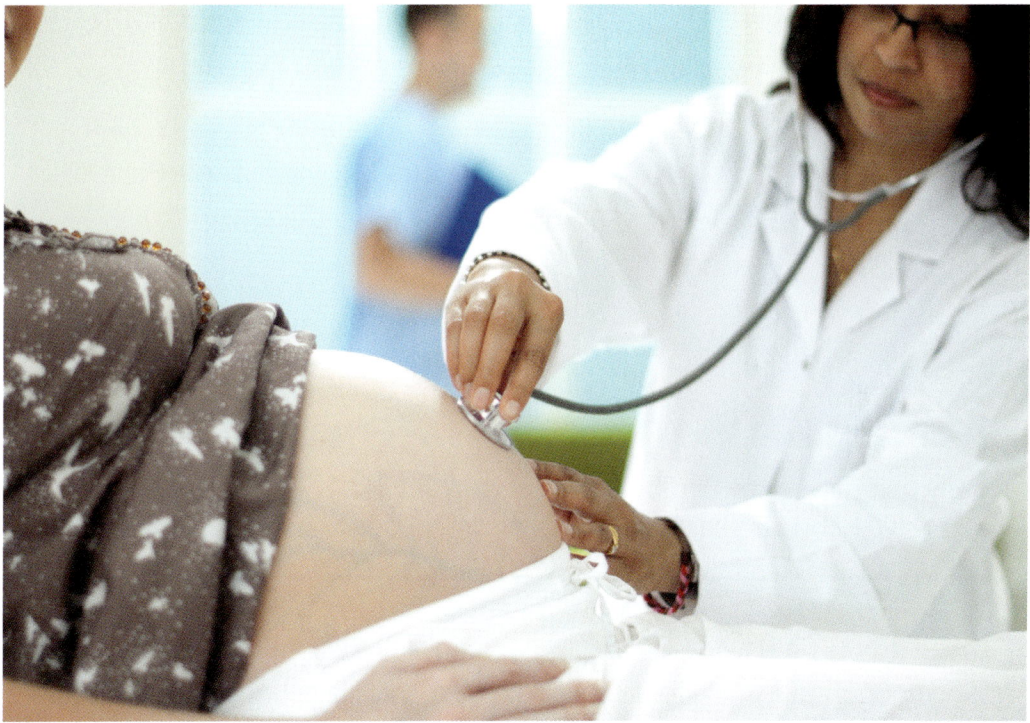

Regular check-ups are very important for all pregnant women.

Counting the Cost

The most important thing all parents can give their children is love. Without love, all the money in the world won't mean very much. That said, it takes a lot more than love to raise a child. Kids are, in fact, startlingly expensive.

The U.S. Department of Agriculture releases an annual estimate of how much it costs to raise children. The researchers look at a number of different costs, including food, housing, transportation, health care, clothing, day care, and more. There is a huge range in the amounts people spend on their kids. For example, spending varies based on whether the family has one parent or two, and also based on the total number of children they have. The age of the child is also important—in general, kids become more expensive the older they get. Where the family lives also plays a role.

The most important factor, however, is the income of the parents. This makes sense—the more income a parent has, the more she or he is likely to spend on children. Among lower-income families, the average spending for each child was around $10,000 per year, whereas for middle-income families, the average was in the neighborhood of $14,000, and among high-income families, the average was around $23,000 per year.

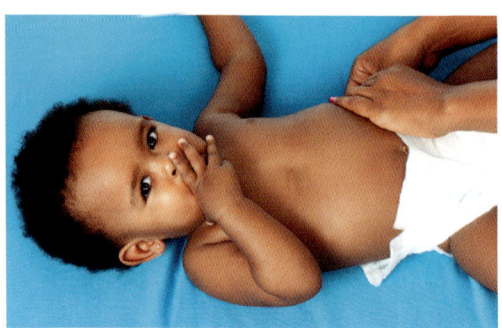

Many parents are startled by how expensive babies actually are.

Pregnant women should be taking prenatal vitamins, eating healthy diets, getting enough rest, and avoiding all drugs, including alcohol and tobacco. They should also be seen by a health-care provider on a regular basis. It does not have

Chapter Two: Being Pregnant

to a doctor necessarily—it could be a midwife or a nurse. Pregnant teens need regular visits with someone who's qualified to check up on both their health and the health of their growing babies. Health-care professionals can also answer questions, explain about what to expect in each stage of pregnancy, and help connect teen moms to social workers if necessary.

CHILDBIRTH AND PARENTING CLASSES

You might have seen a childbirth class portrayed in a film or on TV. The scenes usually involve a roomful of women grunting while men remind them to breathe. The whole thing might seem a bit silly. But that's just on TV. In reality, childbirth classes cover a lot more than just breathing exercises. Subjects include:
- nutrition during pregnancy
- fetal development

Moms-to-be can get a lot of useful information, and possibly even make new friends, in childbirth classes.

- understanding the process of giving birth
- common medical procedures during pregnancy and childbirth
- options for **pain management** during childbirth
- the father's role—before, during, and after the birth
- breast-feeding
- newborn care

Case Study: Terri-Ann

Terri-Ann's 14th birthday was a disaster. She started the day by throwing up. "I thought I just had the stomach flu," she said. "When the doctor said I was pregnant, I started laughing, I didn't believe it was true. By the time [my mom and I] got home, I wasn't laughing anymore, believe me. There was no birthday cake for me that night. I went to bed and cried myself to sleep."

Terri-Ann's pregnancy wasn't an easy one. She was sick to her stomach every day, right through her third trimester. She had just gotten on her school's JV girls' basketball team, but now she had to quit. Her grades went downhill because she missed so much school. Her boyfriend broke up with her, and her mother seemed to be constantly angry at her.

Terri-Ann's baby was born on a cold Saturday night. "I woke up in labor. I was scared stiff. . . . I remember taking [baby Grace] home with mom, how tired I was and how excited at the same time."

Over the next few months, though, Terri-Ann's excitement didn't last. She loved Grace, but she was exhausted all the time. "Grace would be up all night screaming, and I'd want to hold a pillow over her head until she stopped. I'm serious. It terrified me. . . . I went to school, I came home, I took care of Grace, I tried to get some sleep, and then I did it all over again. I never thought life could be so hard."

—Adapted from *Teen Parents* by Rae Simons (Mason Crest, 2010)

Childbirth classes are a key way to help moms of any age prepare themselves for giving birth and caring for a baby. They are especially important for teen moms because it is such a huge leap from *being* a kid to *having* one.

Childbirth classes are also an opportunity to meet other women who are about to become moms. Social support is important for new parents, and childbirth class is the first opportunity to start building that new community. Who knows, your first "mom friend" could be sitting right next to you in childbirth class. (If you need help paying for or getting to childbirth education, talk to your doctor or try the resources at the back of this book.)

Text-Dependent Questions

1. Why is prenatal care important?
2. About how much does a child cost every year?
3. Name at least three things people learn in childbirth class.

Research Project

Find out about childbirth classes in your area—you can do this by searching online or by contacting your local hospital. Ask if they will share a copy of the curriculum with you. Do you agree or disagree that these classes would be useful?

28 Teen Parents

Telling your parents that you're pregnant can be tough—parents often have very different ideas about how they want their daughter's lives to be.

Chapter Three

SPECIAL CONCERNS FOR TEEN MOMS

Every individual is unique, but there are a number of concerns that *most* teenage girls have. These include friends, dating, school, favorite bands, sports and after-school activities, and preparing for college or getting a job. When a girl finds out that she is going to have a baby, all that normal teenage stuff can seem very small. This chapter talks about some of the big challenges and questions that teen moms will have to face.

DEALING WITH OTHERS

Teenage girls who are pregnant don't all feel the same way. They may be happy or not; they may want to keep the baby or not; they may be fearful or even

Words to Understand

cohabitate: live together.

GED: stands for "graduate equivalency diploma"; an accepted stand-in for a high school diploma.

Teen Parents

ashamed. However she feels, there is always that moment when a pregnant teen has to open her mouth and tell someone else what is going on. Whether she's telling her parents or other relatives, her friends, or the baby's father, she should try not take their initial reactions too personally. Often, people will react to the news with a lot of emotion. Those emotions could be pleasant or unpleasant—but in most cases, the initial reaction to the news usually has very little to do with the person delivering it.

Parents. Mom and Dad may be angry at first. That anger could be based in worry about the future, or in disappointment that things haven't turned out the way they hoped. They may also feel guilty—parents often blame themselves for not "protecting" their daughters better. Anger can also mask shame—they might be worrying about what their friends or neighbors will say.

The Father. The baby's father may try to blame the girl for "getting in trouble." He might even deny that the baby is his. Again, this anger is probably more about his own fear—about his future, about the responsibility of parenting, and about the reaction of his friends or parents.

Her Friends. The friends of a pregnant teen will probably have a huge variety of reactions. Some will be sincerely excited for her, and they will eagerly lend their support. Others may worry that they are going to lose their friend to a life of strollers and diapers. Some pregnant teens find that their friends start to pull away or disappear completely. Some are even mean about the pregnancy. That can be hurtful, but it's important to remember that it is probably not a judgment (even if it feels like one!). A lot of times, people avoid others who are going through scary life experiences, but what they're really thinking is, "what if it happens to me?"

Even if these reactions are not very nice, they are all very human. The best advice is to let people have the reactions they are going to have. Let Dad flip out, let Mom cry, give the boyfriend a little space. And then when everyone has calmed down, they will be ready to focus on what's really important: that innocent little baby who is about to arrive.

Chapter Three: Special Concerns for Teen Moms

Help! My BFF is Pregnant

If your friend comes to you with the big news that she's pregnant, what do you do? You want to help, but you also don't want to say the wrong thing. Here are some tips:

- Try not to be judgmental. She is probably pretty embarrassed already.
- Do more listening than talking at first. Let her express herself.
- Remember that this is *her* news to share, not yours. Don't be a gossip.
- Follow through. Check in with her to make sure she's okay and to let her know you haven't dropped her as a friend.
- The most important thing you can do is just love your friend. Let her know that you have her back.

True friends stick together even during hard times.

MARRIAGE AND LIVING TOGETHER

Many people will probably ask a teen mom is she is going to marry the father of the baby. Obviously, a lot depends on the specific situation. The statistics tell us that marriage is fairly unlikely—more than 80 percent of teens who give birth are unmarried.

But if the mother and father are in a relationship, especially if they are in their late teens, it is possible they'll marry, or at least move in together. People may tell you "it's best for the baby," and perhaps that sounds like an old-fashioned thing to say. Evidence does suggest that children who grow up in a home with both parents do better in terms of development and education than those who don't. Fathers tend to be more involved with their kids— emotionally and financially— if they live with the family.

However, young kids who have a negative relationship with their fathers (due to abuse, neglect, or other factors) actually do worse than those who have no relationship at all. So the decision to marry or **cohabitate** should be based on the relationship of the two parents and what is best for the specific people involved. People who are forced into marriage against their will are not likely to stay married very long. Statistics show that marriages that occur when the bride is 23 or over have a much better chance of surviving than those that occur when she is younger.

WORK AND EDUCATION

Once a teen mom has addressed the questions about what she'll do with the baby and how she'll relate to the father, the next big issue is how to support the baby. To work or not to work, that is the question. Many teens choose work, and less than half of pregnant teenagers finish high school.

In fact, there may be a strong impulse to drop out of school and go to work as soon as a girl finds out she is pregnant. This is partly for social reasons. The concerns of a pregnant teens' friends—studying for a history test, or which party

Chapter Three: Special Concerns for Teen Moms

Being in charge of a new life can make regular teenage concerns seem unimportant.

to attend on Saturday—can start to feel pretty silly. She's thinking about bringing a new life into the world, and they are thinking about *prom*? It's easy to see how a girl in that situation might think, *forget those people, I want a job!*

However, it's really important to think long-term. What are the kinds of jobs that are available to high school dropouts? Do they provide opportunities for advancement—meaning more responsibility and more money? Let's be honest: by and large, the jobs that high school dropouts can get are not dream jobs. They do not pay very much money and, importantly, they often don't provide opportunities to grow and make more money later. Yes, it is possible to get lucky, and with a lot of hard work and sacrifice, there can be exceptions. But the general reality, most of the time, is that people without high school diplomas are economically stuck. Meanwhile, as noted

Day Care

Some parents of young children are able to lean on family members for help with child care. Sharing child care with family or close friends is great, but it isn't always possible. That's why so many parents depend on paid child care. Parents—especially moms—may feel guilty about paying strangers to watch their children. That's understandable, but after years of study, the evidence suggests that good day care is not damaging to children, and may even improve their social skills. The key is to find a good day-care center with kind, well-trained staff who will keep children safe when their parents can't be around.

When looking for day care, be sure and visit the place in person and ask a lot of questions. Don't be shy! Here are some things to keep in mind:

- **Licensing.** Make sure that the day care has all the appropriate licenses required by your state.
- **Training.** Ask about how the staff is trained. What activities do they do with the kids? What is their philosophy on discipline if kids misbehave?
- **Setting.** What does the day care look like? Does it seem clean? Does it seem like a pleasant place? Is it over-crowded or very loud?
- **Staff.** Watch how the staff interacts with the kids who are there. Do the people who work there seem to like kids?

Day care can be expensive, but a lot of working moms couldn't get by without it.

Chapter Three: Special Concerns for Teen Moms

in chapter one, babies just get more expensive as they get older.

That history test might seem kind of pointless in the short term. Maybe it seems selfish for a girl to think about her own education when she could be earning money for her baby. But earning a high school diploma is not a selfish act: it's something she does *for* her baby, so that she can build a better life.

Kids learn what is important in life by watching their parents. By staying in school or by going back for a **GED**, a teen mom is showing her child that education matters. A diploma is far from selfish—it is the best gift a teen mom can give her child.

About 40 percent of teen mothers finish high school.

Text-Dependent Questions

1. What kinds of reactions can a teen mom expect from her friends and family?
2. Why is a high school diploma important?
3. What are some things to look for in a good day care?

Research Project

Find job listings in your local area. Make a list of the different job postings you see and what education the jobs require. (If the information is not included in the posting, call the company and ask.) Create a list of starting salaries and the education levels that companies require. What does this show you?

Teen Parents

Can teens be good parents? Of course they can! But nobody says it will be easy.

Chapter Four

BEING A MOM, BEING A DAD

Babies are cute. They are really, really cute. They smell great (usually), they make adorable noises, and they love their moms like nobody else. Some moms feel that nobody has ever loved them quite the way their baby does.

As humans, we are designed to love and protect our little ones. It is an instinct that has been passed down for thousands of years. Even back when humans lived in caves, the more that parents loved their children, the more likely those parents would be to give them the last bit of food or protect them from saber-toothed tigers.

But there's another reason why we are so naturally devoted. Parental instinct is what keeps us from hurting our babies when they keep us awake, scream for hours, make messes, break stuff, and generally make us furious. Even the most

Words to Understand

alienating: something that makes you feel separate from everyone else.
paternity: fatherhood.
stereotype: a quick assumption about an individual based on outside factors.

loving mom has, at least once, had a fantasy about returning her kid to the hospital for a refund. As cute and cuddly as a baby can be, that same baby will sometimes drive his or her parents *completely crazy*.

Parenting is not an easy job for anyone. And some people are better at it than others. It's possible for a 16-year-old to be a patient, fantastic parent, just as it's possible for a 36-year-old to be a selfish, lousy one. But in general, the younger a parent is, the tougher it can be for him or her to set aside personal needs and put the child first.

Are you ever . . .

- in a bad mood?
- feeling sick?
- mad at your partner?
- stressed about work (or homework)?

Guess what? The baby doesn't care. Not even a little. And it's not the baby's job to care. People who study child development tell us that kids don't even understand that other people have points of view until they are about three or four years old. It's the parents' job to put aside all those grown-up concerns and focus on what their children need.

SOME WORDS ON TEEN DADS

Books about teen parents tend to focus a lot on girls. It's easy to understand why. After all, it's the girl who has to carry the baby. It's the girl whose body and life are turned upside down by the pregnancy. But the girl wouldn't even be in that situation without the boy. So while pregnancy might seem like "a girl thing," it really isn't. Pregnancy, childbirth, and parenting are concerns for *anyone* who is interested in the opposite sex.

Getting the News. Boys who suddenly become fathers are in a difficult position. Although they don't experience the physical changes of pregnancy, fathers do feel some of that same shock when they get the news. They may feel angry

Chapter Four: Being a Mom, Being a Dad 39

Teen fathers have the right to be involved in their children's lives. But they also have responsibilities.

or worried . . . or they may not know *what* to feel. The truth is, pregnancy can be very **alienating** for men of any age. On the one hand, the father is clearly involved because it's his baby, too. But in another sense, he is not at all involved. After all, pregnancy is mostly out of his control. The instant shift from "I am a boy" to "I am a father" can be very confusing.

There can be a strong temptation to deny responsibility and just pretend the pregnancy isn't happening. After all, there is no morning sickness or weight gain to constantly remind the father that a baby is on the way. An additional complication occurs when the dad-to-be does not have a relationship with his own father. Considering the fact that about 35 percent of kids are currently being raised in single-parent families, this is not so rare. It can be all too easy for a young father-to-be to "just not think about it."

That's an understandable impulse, but it is not a very admirable one. Fathers-to-be are every bit as responsible as mothers-to-be. And even if the father chooses to forget about the pregnancy, he should be aware that the government will not. Fathers, even underage ones, can always be held legally responsible for child support.

Stepping Up. Fortunately, the evidence suggests that more and more young fathers are "stepping up" and taking responsibility. The **stereotype** of the disinterested teen dad is becoming just that, an incorrect stereotype.

How does a young father-to-be learn the skills he needs to be a good father to his child? The advice given in chapter four also applies here: don't go it alone. It won't be easy, however, because there are not as many social services available for teen fathers as there are for mothers. Partly that's because it's very easy to know who the pregnant teenagers are, but figuring out who the fathers are is not as obvious. **Paternity** can be hard to establish, which makes fathers harder to count. Also, there are simply fewer teen dads than there are teen moms: about 20 percent of teen pregnancies involve a male over the age of 20.

Fortunately, the lack of attention to dads is changing. For example, the National Responsible Fatherhood Clearinghouse (www.fatherhood.gov) offers information and advice for fathers, as well as information about in-person fatherhood training programs around the country. Teen dads need support, advice, and encouragement, just like teen moms do. They need educations and job skills, just like teen moms do. They need to improve their parenting and communication skills. Just like teen moms, teen dads need to put their kids' needs first. And sometimes the most manly thing a person can do is ask for help.

Chapter Four: Being a Mom, Being a Dad

Read, Dad, Read

New moms get a lot of "bonding time" with their babies. This bonding especially happens when the baby is fed. There is something about curling up with a baby to feed it that's very cozy and loving. Fathers don't always get to enjoy this time (although some can, if their babies are bottle-fed). But there is one great way that dads can get that same bonding in: by sitting down with a book and reading out loud.

You might be thinking, "What difference does reading make? It's not like a baby can understand what I'm saying!" Well, that's true, but it's also not true. The baby might not understand each word, but he or she does learn some very important things. First, the baby learns that dad cares. Paying attention to your kids lets them know that they matter. And reading to your baby shows that reading matters, too. If Dad does something repeatedly, it must be important, right? That's how young kids think.

What you are reading doesn't actually matter very much. Picture books are great, but if you like to read about sports, do that. It's fine—your baby just wants to be with you.

Study after study has shown that young children who are read to at home will have better language skills and do better in school.

Teen Parents

Sometimes parents feel frustrated that they are missing out on fun things because of their kids. It may help to know that all parents feel this way sometimes, not just teenage parents.

CONCLUSION: TWO THINGS AT ONCE

Adolescence is a stage of child development. It's meant to be a transition into adulthood. Through experimentation (and sometimes rebellion), teens figure out who they are and what kind of lives they want.

When a teenage girl gets pregnant, she—and her partner—have to jump past a lot of that development and dive straight into adulthood. Babies are basically just helpless bundles of need, and caring for them is a tough job. But it can be done, and it can be done well. Teen parents need support from their families, friends, and communities. Don't be afraid to ask for help! You deserve it, and so does your baby.

Chapter Four: Being a Mom, Being a Dad

Text-Dependent Questions

1. How old does a child have to be before he or she realizes that other people are separate individuals with their own feelings?
2. What kinds of emotions might a boy go through when he learns he is about to be a father?
3. Why is reading to babies important?

Research Project

Pick out a couple of your favorite picture books from when you were younger, and offer to read them to a kindergarten class at your school. (Alternatively, you could volunteer for a few hours in your school or public library, and offer to read to kids there.) Afterwards, write about what it felt like to read to those kids. Did you like it, or not? How did the kids respond to the books you chose?

FURTHER READING

Books

Goyer, Trisha. *Life Interrupted: The Scoop on Being a Young Mom.* Grand Rapids, MI: Zondervan, 2004.

Haskins-Bookser, Laura. *Dreams to Reality: Help for Young Moms; Education, Career, and Life Choices.* Buena Park, CA: Morning Glory Press, 2006.

Lindsay, Jeanne Warren. *Teen Dads: Rights, Responsibilities, and Joys.* Rev. ed. Buena Park, CA: Morning Glory Press, 2008.

Williams-Wheeler, Dorrie. *The Unplanned Pregnancy Book for Teens and College Students.* Virginia Beach, VA: Sparkledoll Productions, 2003.

Online

Boonstra, Heather D. "What Is Behind the Declines in Teen Pregnancy Rates?" *Guttmacher Policy Review* 17, no. 3 (Summer 2014). http://www.guttmacher.org/pubs/gpr/17/3/gpr170315.html.

Healthy Children. "Teen Parents." https://www.healthychildren.org/English/ages-stages/teen/dating-sex/Pages/Teen-Parents.aspx.

One Tough Job. http://www.onetoughjob.org/.

Get Help Now

Housing Hope: Teen Parent Program

Information and help for teen parents who are homeless or at risk of becoming homeless.

http://www.housinghope.org/programs/teenParent.html

SERIES GLOSSARY

agencies: departments of a government with responsibilities for specific programs.

anxiety: a feeling of worry or nervousness.

biological parents: the woman and man who create a child; they may or not raise it.

caregiving: helping someone with their daily activities.

cognitive: having to do with thinking or understanding.

consensus: agreement among a particular group of people.

custody: legal guardianship of a child.

demographers: people who study information about people and communities.

depression: severe sadness or unhappiness that does not go away easily.

discrimination: singling out a group for unfair treatment.

disparity: a noticeable difference between two things.

diverse: having variety; for example, "ethnically diverse" means a group of people of many different ethnicities.

ethnicity: a group that has a shared cultural heritage.

extended family: the kind of family that includes members beyond just parents and children, such as aunts, uncles, cousins, and so on.

foster care: raising a child (usually temporarily) that is not adopted or biologically yours.

heir: someone who receives another person's wealth and social position after the other person dies.

homogenous: a group of things that are the same.

ideology: a set of ideas and ways of seeing the world.

incarceration: being confined in prison or jail.

inclusive: accepting of everyone.

informally: not official or legal.

institution: an established organization, custom, or tradition.

kinship: family relations.

neglect: not caring for something correctly.

patriarchal: a system that is run by men and fathers.

prejudice: beliefs about a person or group based only on simplified and often mistaken ideas.

prevalence: how common a particular trait is in a group of people.

psychological: having to do with the mind.

quantify: to count or measure objectively.

restrictions: limits on what someone can do.

reunification: putting something back together.

secular: nonreligious.

security: being free from danger.

social worker: a person whose job is to help families or children deal with particular problems.

socioeconomic: relating to both social factors (such as race and ethnicity) as well as financial factors (such as class).

sociologists: people who study human society and how it operates.

spectrum: range.

stability: the sense that things will stay the same.

stereotype: a simplified idea about a type of person that is not connected to actual individuals.

stigma: a judgment that something is bad or shameful.

stressor: a situation or event that causes upset (stress).

traumatic: something that's very disturbing and causes long-term damage to a person.

variable: something that can change.

INDEX

Page numbers in *italics* refer to photographs or tables.

abortion   16–17, 22–23

abstinence   17–19

abstinence-only programs   18–19

adoption   23

anemia   21, 23

birth control   *15*, 18–19

   myths about   13

childbirth class   25–27

children, cost of   24

cohabitation   29, 32

day care   24, 34

fathers   22, 26, 30, 32, 38–41, *42*

friends   29-30, 31

GED (graduate equivalency degree)   35

high blood pressure   23

marriage   32

National Responsible Fatherhood Clearinghouse   40

parenting challenges   37–38, 42

pregnancy, teen   13, *18*, 19, *20*, 21–25,

   international rates of   16–17

   school and   32–35

   telling people about   22, 29–30

   U.S. rates of   14–15, 16–17, 18–19

prenatal care   23–25

reading, importance of   41

Sanger, Margaret   15

sexual activity, pressure about   12–14

sexual activity, rates of   11–14

sexually transmitted infections (STIs)   12, 15, 18

teen parents

   education and   32–35

   friends and   30, 31, 32–33

virginity pledges   18

ABOUT THE AUTHOR

H. W. Poole is a writer and editor of books for young people, including the 13-volume set, *Mental Illnesses and Disorders: Awareness and Understanding* (Mason Crest). She created the *Horrors of History* series (Charlesbridge) and the *Ecosystems* series (Facts On File). She has also been responsible for many critically acclaimed reference books, including *Political Handbook of the World* (CQ Press) and the *Encyclopedia of Terrorism* (SAGE). She was coauthor and editor of *The History of the Internet* (ABC-CLIO), which won the 2000 American Library Association RUSA award.

PHOTO CREDITS

Photos are for illustrative purposes only; individuals depicted are models.
Cover: Dollar Photo Club/razyph
iStock.com: 6 MordorIff; 9 Den Kuvaiev; 10 camptown; 19 KatarzynaBialasiewicz; 20 sturti; 23 sturti; 24 RussianDashinsky; 25 Halfpoint; 28 Juanmonino; 31 FlairImages; 33 quavondo; 34 Jonas unruh; 35 jeebbus; 36 Justin Horrocks; 39 RubyRain
Library of Congress: 15
Shutterstock: 41 iofoto; 42 oliveromg
Wikimedia Commons: 12 Justin McIntosh; 18 lunar caustic

SANDUSKY LIBRARY   NOV   2016